Purpose Struggles?

Don Barnes

Published by Don Barnes, 2024.

This publication provides the Author's opinion and neither the publisher or the author intends to render legal, accounting, or other professional advice with this publication.
The publisher and the author disclaim any personal liability, loss or risk incurred as a consequence of the use and application, with directly or indirectly, of an advice, information or methods presented in this publication.

First Edition

Copyright © 2025
By Don Barnes / Tryune Works!

TRYUNE WORKS! and Life works in threes are trademarks and copyrights of Don Barnes and Tryune Works!

LifeWorksInThrees.com

Table of Contents

About the Author

Don is the founder and author of Life Works in Threes!™ E-books. He is a lifelong Texan who has traveled extensively while taking a keen interest in human behavior. His curiosity about life and what drives humans led him to the discovery of how life works in threes. He coined this term as the *Tryune Concept.*

Don attended college on an athletic scholarship and then embarked on a 30-year career in the oil and gas industry. Since the year 2000, he has been a consultant for distributors and manufacturers of various industries. Along the way, he worked on his Tryune discovery in hopes of someday sharing his findings with those struggling unnecessarily... in life. What Don surmised from 40+ years of R&D was that people were struggling unnecessarily because they were not aware that "life works in threes." They, for the most part, have been living their lives by chance rather than by choice, he also discovered.

From this, he began focusing on the "mechanics of life" which shows formulas for success with subjects such as *life, health, money, purpose and so forth*. When people are able to grasp the Tryune Concept, they can apply the formulas with topics that interest them and begin eliminating the struggle. This epiphany is what triggered his Tryune venture and is now on the path of sharing with all who desire to improve on their lives.

Don currently resides in Southern California and Texas while overseeing his businesses and investments.

Life Works in Threes™

When I was a kid growing up, no one sat me down and said, "Okay Don, I'm going to show you how life works so that you can navigate your way through adulthood." I graduated from school, got married and went about my way with the "learn as you go" concept. It was kind of like putting together a backyard swing set without a set of instructions. Lots of frustration and do-overs, for sure!

My discovery of the "triune" word and noticing how things come together in threes is really what set me off on researching that maybe "life comes in three" ...sort of a mechanical approach to managing life, if you will. I combed the libraries and bookstores for information on this and found one book on the subject that was written back in 1951. The author's name was John S. Arant.

What Mr. Arant had to say is this "For lack of a better name, I have called this *The Triangle of Triumph* and therefore, consistent with the name, since most of these conclusions are built on the geometric figure of the triangle." He continued "All Life and all lives are seated in, and circumscribed by, the triangle. The Author and Source and Director of all life is Himself triune in character – Father, Son, and Holy Spirit. Man is of triple nature – body, mind, and spirit   and within those three there are many triangles – desires, development, decay; intellect, will, sensibilities. Of this "paced interlude in the midst of eternity" which we call time there is the triangle of Past, Present, and Future. Space – that limitless and measureless element of the physical universe – is best known in terms of Height, Breadth, and Depth. Try building yourself some triangles along the lines of your Will, your Work, your Way – You will find some interesting angles.

So, for the first time, I realized that life is designed in a mechanical way to come in threes. That means you don't have to rely on wishing and hoping things turn out okay. You can actually look at the three parts that a particular thing is made of and then apply them to get what you're wanting. Like a three-ingredient recipe or a combination lock. With a combination lock, you need the three exact numbers to unlock the lock...otherwise you will continue to struggle.

Some 40 years later, I accumulated things that work in threes and that's when I knew I needed to share this with anyone wanting answers. To have success/harmony in your life, just apply the three parts of an area you're working on, and things will fall into place. I also learned that the recipe for success with just about anything is by doing these three things, consistently – THINK positively, SPEAK positively and ACT positively. For example, if I want to be a successful artist. I would think to myself "I can do this because I have the talent." Then I would speak it this way "Yes, I am working on my art degree and plan to do portraits professionally." Finally, I would act on that by taking art classes and continue crafting my skill. Eventually, I will see the positive results/ success I'm looking for.

Conversely, if I think positively but speak negatively...it will cancel out. Or if I speak positively but have no positive action going on...nothing will happen.

I looked up "How Life Works" and "The Mechanics of Life" and these are really talking about the biology of how our cells work and other chemistry. Life Works in Threes! teaches that life is kind of like building blocks. Pick a topic you may be struggling with. See the three parts that topic consists of and then start applying them...on a consistent basis. That will help you overcome the struggle and get you back in harmony/ success with how life works.

For 30+ years I was a golf instructor (by accident). My two kids had some success playing junior golf and so friends and neighbors would ask me to show them and their kids how to play golf successfully. From all of this, I got pretty good at watching golfers on the driving range and could spot right away why they were struggling with hitting bad golf shots. I was able to do that because I knew the three steps to hitting good golf shots. I learned them from studying golf and played for several decades. I "broke the code" for me so to speak.

So now you know that life works in threes. You can live your life *by choice* rather than *by chance* and that my friend... is the key to a fulfilling life.

LIFE WORKS
IN THREES!

My sanctuary on the Pacific coast

Introduction

Living by choice and living by chance are two contrasting approaches to life, each with its own set of implications and outcomes. When we choose to live by choice, we actively engage with our decisions, steering our lives in directions aligned with our values, goals, and aspirations. It's like being the captain of our own ship, navigating through the vast sea of possibilities with purpose and intention. This approach empowers us to take ownership of our destiny, fostering a sense of autonomy and fulfillment along the way.

On the other hand, living by chance is akin to drifting aimlessly on a raft, at the mercy of unpredictable currents and external circumstances. While it may offer a sense of spontaneity and adventure, it also entails surrendering control over our lives to random happenstance. Opportunities may arise by happenstance rather than design, and outcomes become subject to the whims of fate. While this approach can lead to unexpected discoveries and serendipitous moments, it can also leave us feeling powerless and unsure of where life will take us next.

In essence, living by choice empowers us to shape our own destinies, while living by chance entails surrendering control to the uncertainties of fate. While both approaches have their merits, consciously making choices allows us to craft lives that are more aligned with our values, desires, and aspirations. So, whether we prefer to chart our course or let the winds of fortune guide us, embracing a balance of choice and chance can enrich our lives with purpose, meaning, and fulfillment.

My discovery of the Tryune Concept

Before we dive into purpose struggles and how to overcome them, let me share my discovery of the Tryune concept and how life works in threes. It all began in the summer of 1982.

I grew up with parents who treated everyone with decency and respect. My three older sisters and I were raised in a home that was "middle-class traditional." We lived in modest homes in different small towns, attended school and church on a regular basis and celebrated all the traditional holidays. Eventually we settled during the spring of 1964 in the big city of Houston, Texas. I'll never forget the vastness of the city and hearing sirens from police cars, fire trucks and ambulances on a regular basis. I was excited and scared at the same time.

Once settled in this fast-paced city, I finished my growing-up years with an academic diploma and sweetheart intact. I got a job, bought a car, got married, bought a house and produced two beautiful babies in a span of about 5 years. Talk about having to grow up fast!

Things went from great in my childhood to absolute misery in my young adulthood. I began to struggle with my job because deep down I just hated what I was doing. This problem created a snowball effect because soon after, my weight, my finances, my relationships, my happiness and everything else worth saving was going down the drain. I eventually hit a level of frustration that I had never experienced before and didn't know how to get out of it. My cry for help was for anyone or anything to come to my rescue. I just ran out of solutions for my situation.

This is when my discovery happened.

One night shortly after my meltdown, while sleeping soundly, the word "triune" began to softly pound in my head like a mantra. I woke up a little startled and decided to go look up the word in my favorite dictionary (this was WAY before Google.) The definition said '**triune** (try-une) – 1) a group of three things; united. 2) Being 3 in 1 such as *humans are mental, physical and spiritual.* I scratched my head, got a glass of water and went back to bed.

The next day while driving around town, I began thinking about things that I was taught in my younger years that came in threes. My Boy Scout manual taught that to have **character**, I needed to be *1) physically strong,* 2) *mentally awake and 3) morally straight.* My high school football coach would say emphatically "If you want to be **a good football player**, you have to be *1) mobile 2) agile and 3) hostile!*" My first sales manager shared with me that to be **a successful salesman**, I needed to have *1) sales skills, 2) product knowledge and 3) a good image.*

"Hmm", I thought, "wonder if there are other examples out there of things that work in threes?" So, some 40 years later, I have researched and discovered that many, many things work in threes. What this message was telling me is that to achieve success or balance in any significant area of my life, the three things that area consisted of had to be present continuously. That's when I had my epiphany. This discovery was telling me the secret to how life <u>really</u> works.

Tryune is a play on the word "triune" as an invitation to "try" this concept. Furthermore, we do not say that life <u>only</u> works in threes. Life also works in ones, twos, fours and so on. What has been observed though is that the many things significant to life, just so happen to come and work in threes. That's what is being shared in this book.

Now, you are about to see 40+ years of research and proof that life works in threes. I did not make up any of these topics. I invite you to research them on the internet, as I did, to validate what is written here. There are some interesting facts that most of us have never realized...until now.

How Life Works in Threes (around 200 examples)

<u>LIFE</u>

DON BARNES

Humans consist of *body, mind and soul.*

A human's basic needs are *health, income and provisions.*

A human's basic wants are *comfort, gain and approval.*

Our minds are made up of the *conscious, the subconscious and the unconscious.*

Philosophy explains *the id, the ego and superego.*

Atoms consist of *protons, neutrons and electrons.*

Motion is explained by *three basic laws.*

Science falls under three main branches: *natural, social and formal sciences*

Time is *past, present and future...*at the same time.

Electricity consists of *ohms, amperes and voltage.*

Music's basic elements are *duration, pitch and timbre.*

Democracy is a government *of the people, by the people and for the people.*

U.S. branches of government are *the judicial, the executive and the legislative.*

Armed Forces protect us on *land, air and sea.*

Environmentally, we are asked *to reduce, recycle and re-use.*

The news program gives us *the news, sports and conditions.*

Our days consist of *morning, afternoon and evening.*

Three months in each season of the year

Our main meals are known as *breakfast, lunch and dinner.*

A balanced diet consists of *good proteins, carbohydrates and fats.*

Traditional Family consists of *father, mother, and child(ren)*

<u>SCIENCES</u>

Three major branches of natural science – *(physical, earth/ space and life sciences)*

Three major branches of modern physics - *(classical, relativistic, quantum)*

Three major branches of biology *(botany, zoology, microbiology)*

Three spatial dimensions: *height* (up/down), *width* (left/ right) and *depth* (forwards/backwards)

Three-gauge bosons (photon, gluon, W&Z bosons)

Three types of elementary particles *(leptons, quarks, gauge bosons)*

Three quarks in every proton *(two "up" and one "down")*

Three primary colors of light *(red, green, blue)*

Three color tone properties *(hue, value, chroma)*

Three laws of motion (*Newton's laws*)

Three laws of planetary motion (*Kepler's laws*)

Three layers of the Sun's interior (*core, radiative zone, convective zone*)

Three layers of the Sun's atmosphere (*photosphere, chromosphere, corona*)

Three types of meteorites (*iron, stony iron, stony*)

Three types of galaxy shapes (*elliptical, spiral, irregular*)

Three substances of the universe (*normal matter, 'dark matter', 'dark energy'*)

Three phases of the moon (*new moon, first quarter, full moon*)

Three planetary regions (*temperate, sub-tropical, tropical*)

Three layers of the Earth (*crust, mantle, core*)

Three components of an ecosystem (*producers, consumers, decomposers*)

Three types of rocks (*igneous, sedimentary, metamorphic*)

Three types of fossil fuels (*coal, crude oil, natural gas*)

Three hydrological processes (*evaporation, condensation, precipitation*)

Three basic types of (meteorological) precipitation (*liquid, freezing, frozen*)

Three types of substances *(mono-constituent, multi-constituent, UVCB)*

Three phases of (normal) matter *(solid, liquid, gas)*

Three types of covalent chemical bonds *(single, double and triple bonds)*

Three isotopes of hydrogen *(protium, deuterium, tritium)*

Three atoms in each molecule of water *(two hydrogen atoms and an oxygen atom)*

Three endings to salts *(-ide, -ite, -ate)*

Three requirements for fire *(fuel, oxygen, heat)*

Three nucleotide bases in a genetic codon

Three domains of life *(archaea, bacteria and eukaryotes)*

Three major groups of flowering plants *(monocots, eudicots, magnolids)*

Three major functions that are basic to plant growth and development: *(photosynthesis* [making sugars], *respiration* [metabolizing those sugars], and *transpiration* [water vapor loss]

Three things that the chlorophyll in plants needs for photosynthesis to take place: *(sunlight, carbon dioxide and water)*

Transpiration serves three roles: *(cooling the plant, moving minerals* and *sugars through the plant,* and *maintaining the turgidity pressure* [stiffness] *of the plant's cells)*

Three parts of an insect's body *(head, thorax, abdomen)*

<u>BIOLOGY</u>

Three types of cones in the retina, relating to the three primary colors

Three semi-circular canals in the ear *(lateral, anterior, posterior)*

Three sections in the ear *(outer, middle, inner)*

Three ossicles in the middle ear *(malleus, incus, stapes)*

Three segments to each limb *(proximal, mid, distal)*

Three bones in each arm *(humerus, radius, ulna)*

Three joints in the arm *(shoulder, elbow, wrist)*

Three joints in the leg *(hip, knee, ankle)*

Three joints in the elbow *(humeroulnar, humeroradial, proximal radioulnar)*

Three functional compartments in the knee joint *(the femoropatellar, medial femorotibial* and *lateral femorotibial articulations)*

Three types of fibrous joints *(sutures, gomphoses, syndesmoses)*

Three types of bone in each hand (*carpals, metacarpals, phalanges*)

Three types of bone in each foot (*tarsals, metatarsals, phalanges*)

Three bones (phalanges) in each finger and in each toe (*proximal, intermediate, distal*)

Three layers of skin (*dermis, epidermis, hypodermis*)

Three components of a cell (*cell membrane, nucleus, cytoplasm*)

Three types of blood vessels (*arteries, veins, capillaries*)

Three types of blood cells [*red* (erythrocytes), *white* (leukocytes), *platelets* (thrombocytes)]

Three processes of the intestinal tract (*ingestion, digestion, excretion*)

Three germ layers (*Endoderm, Mesoderm, Ectoderm*)

Three parts of a human tooth (*crown, neck, root*)

Three organs of otolaryngology (*ear, nose, throat*)

Three major body systems (*digestive, circulatory, respiratory*)

Three parts to a neuron: (*soma* [*cell body*], *axon, dendrites*)

Three main parts of the brain (*forebrain, midbrain, hindbrain*)

Three parts of the forebrain (*cerebrum, thalamus, hypothalamus*)

Three parts of the midbrain (*colliculi, tegmentum, cerebral peduncles*)

Three parts of the hindbrain (*cerebellum, pons, medulla*)

Three membranes enclosing the brain (*dura mater, arachnoid, pia mater*)

The brain operates on three levels: *consciously* (for cognitive thought and declarative memory); *subconsciously* (for pre-planned actions and procedural memory); and *unconsciously* (for breathing, heart beating, etc.)

Our conscious mind is fed from three sources: *our senses* (which can be fooled); *our memory* (which is flawed); and *our imagination* (which is inventive)

Three aspects of the human mind (*memory, intellect, will*)

Three parts of the human personality (*id, ego, superego*)

The sum of human capacity consists of three abilities (*thought, word and deed*)

Three times of man (*birth, life, death*)

Three periods of the Gait Cycle (*initial double limb support, single limb support, and terminal double limb support*)

MUSIC

Three types of musical notes (*sharps, flats, naturals*)

Three aspects of a song (*lyrics, melody, rhythm*)

Three types of musical chords (*root, third, fifth*)

<u>MATHEMATICS</u>

Three types of a real number (*positive, negative, zero*)

Three parts to any arithmetic operation: for addition: *augend, addend and sum* - for subtraction: *minuend, subtrahend and difference* - for multiplication: *multiplicand, multiplier and product* - for division: *dividend, divisor and quotient*

Three laws of arithmetic operations (*commutative, associative, distributive*)

Three types of equivalence relation (*reflexivity, symmetry, transitivity*)

Three types of symmetry operations (*translation, rotation, reflection*)

Three geometries (*Euclidean, spherical, hyperbolic*)

The number 3 is the basis of an entire branch of mathematics, called trigonometry (from the Greek *trigonon* "triangle" + *metron* "measure")

Three trigonometric functions (*sine, cosine, tangent*)

Three types of average (*mean, mode, median*)

<u>GRAMMAR</u>

Three logical operators (*AND, OR and NOT*)

Three laws of logic (*identity, noncontradiction, excluded middle*)

Three parts of a logical syllogism (*major premise, minor premise, conclusion*)

Three grammatical parts to a sentence (*subject, verb, complement*)

Three persons in grammar [*1st person* (I/we), *2nd* (you or your), *3rd* (he/she/it/they)]

Three genders in grammar [*masculine* (he/him), *feminine* (she/her), *neuter* (it)]

Three forms of comparison in grammar [*positive, comparative* (more, -er), *superlative* (most, -est)]

Three cases in (English) grammar [*subjective/nominative* (he), *objective/accusative* (him) and *possessive/genitive* (his)]

Three parts of a narrative (*beginning, middle, end*)

Components of an essay (*introduction, body, conclusion*)

Elements of a rhetorical appeal (*ethos, pathos, logos*)

Aspects of a story (*plot, characters, setting*)

<u>RELIGION</u>

The Creator – *omniscient, omnipotent, omnipresent*

Christian God – *Father, Son, Holy Spirit*

Jesus – *The Way, The Truth, The Life*

Ancient Near East- *Qudshu, Astarte, Anat*

Classical Antiquity – Many dieties came in threes

Hinduism – Para Brahman is *Brahma, Visnu, Shiva*

Ancient Celtic Cultures – *many example of triad dieties*

Buddhism – *The three jewels*

Taoism – *The three pure ones*

Islam – *Fear, Hope and Love*

Baha'i - *Intention, Power and Action*

Confucianism – *Benevolence, Wisdom and Courage*

<u>OTHER TRIUNE EXAMPLES</u>

3 Coins in a Fountain

3 Days of the Condor

3 Miles in a League

3 Goals in a Hat Trick

3 Piece Suit

3 Feet in a Yard

3 Books in Lord of the Rings

3 Ring Circus

3 Ships of Christopher Columbus

3 Sheets to the Wind

3 Books in a Trilogy

3 Wheels on a Tricycle

3 Wise Men

3-Legged Race

3 Ring Circus

3-Wheeler

3 Cornered Hat

3 Dimensional

3 Musketeers

3 R's (reading, 'riting, 'rithmatic)

3 Sides of a triangle

3 Races in the Triple Crown (horse racing)

3 Angles in a Triangle

3 Trimesters in a Pregnancy

3 Flavors in Neapolitan Ice Cream

3 Stars in Orion's belt

3 Barleycorns in an Inch

3 Hands on a Clock (with the Seconds Hand)

3 Colors in a Flag

3 Minute Egg

3 Great Pyramids at Giza

3 Holes in a Bowling Ball

3 Colors in a Set of Traffic Lights

3 Minutes in a Boxing Round

3 Teaspoons in a Tablespoon

3 Legs on a Stool

3 Monastic Vows (Obience, Stability, Conversatio Morum)

3 Body Types: Endomorph, Mesomorph, Ectomorph

3 Ring Notebooks

3 Germ layers: Endoderm, Mesoderm, Ectoderm

3 Species of Homo: Homo habilis, Homo erectus, Homo sapiens

3 Basic parts of a camera: Lens, Shutter, Sensor

3 Stages of a Project lifecycle: initiation, planning, execution

The Truth, The Whole Truth and Nothing but the Truth

Life, Liberty and the Pursuit of Happiness

Hear no Evil, See no Evil, Speak no Evil

National motto of France/Haiti: Liberty, Equality, Fraternity

Paper, Rock, Scissors

Ready, Aim, Fire

On Your mark, Get Set, Go

Olympic medals of gold, silver, bronze

Types of joints (ball & socket, hinge, pivot)

Stages of a rocket launch (launch, orbit, re-entry)

Parts of a joke (setup, delivery, punchline)

Primary components of a transistor (emitter, base, collector)

Primary components of an airplane (fuselage, wings, empennage)

Basic components of a computer: CPU, memory, storage

Three phases in the development of technology (*eotechnic* [*mechanical*], *paleotechnic* [*steam-powered*] and *neotechnic* [*electric-powered*]

Communication systems require three components (*transmitter, channel, receiver*)

The list goes on. See if you can find more examples as they are everywhere in our universe! Now that you know that life works in threes (with proof!), we can begin to apply this concept to whatever topics we want.

So, to overcome struggles with purpose, we need to apply the three areas that purpose consists of – TALENTS, VALUES and NEEDS. We'll start with TALENTS:

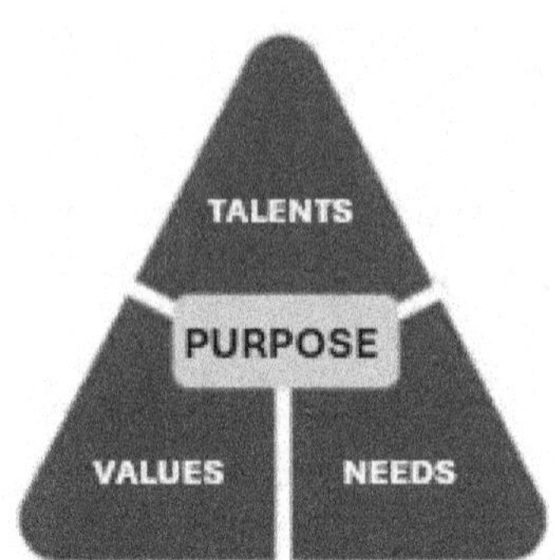

TALENTS
PURPOSE
VALUES
NEEDS

PURPOSE

Purpose can be defined as the reason for which something is done or created, or for which something exists. It is the intended goal or desired result that drives an individual or entity to take action, make decisions, or pursue certain objectives. Purpose often implies a sense of meaning, direction, and significance in one's actions or existence. It can vary from personal purposes such as career goals or life missions to broader purposes such as the objectives of organizations or the meaning of life itself.

Purpose is like a companion that grows and evolves with us as we journey through life. When we're young, our sense of purpose might be closely tied to immediate goals or dreams—like becoming an astronaut, a doctor, or an artist. It's often driven by curiosity, passion, or what we think will make us happy. As we gain experiences and learn more about ourselves and the world, our purpose can shift. What once seemed like the ultimate goal may no longer hold the same allure or significance. We start to see new opportunities or challenges that reshape our understanding of what truly matters to us.

Sometimes, life throws unexpected curveballs our way—whether it's a change in career, a new relationship, or a personal revelation—that can completely alter our sense of purpose. These moments of reflection and adaptation are crucial as we navigate the twists and turns of life. Our purpose becomes more nuanced and layered, influenced by our evolving values, priorities, and the relationships we cherish. Ultimately, purpose isn't a static destination but a dynamic journey of discovery and growth, where each chapter adds depth and meaning to our lives.

I used to think that I had to "find" my purpose but learned later on that it is up to us to "create" our purpose. It made all the difference for my peace of mind.

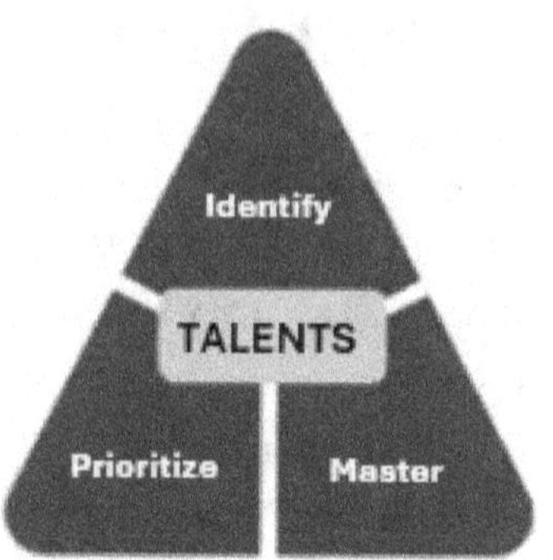
Identify
TALENTS
Prioritize
Master

TALENTS

Humans are born with an astonishing array of natural talents, each as unique as the individual themselves. From the moment we enter the world, we carry within us an innate potential waiting to be discovered and nurtured. These talents encompass a wide spectrum, ranging from artistic flair and musical aptitude to analytical prowess and athletic ability. They're like gifts bestowed upon us, ready to be unwrapped and explored as we journey through life.

One of the most fascinating aspects of natural talents is their diversity and variability. Just as no two fingerprints are alike, no two individuals possess exactly the same set of innate abilities. Some may excel in creative endeavors, effortlessly painting masterpieces or composing beautiful melodies, while others may thrive in scientific inquiry, unraveling the mysteries of the universe with keen intellect and curiosity. These talents often reveal themselves early in life, manifesting in childhood interests and inclinations that shape our paths as we grow and develop.

Natural talents have the remarkable capacity to evolve and grow with us over time. While we may be born with certain predispositions, the extent to which we cultivate and refine these talents is largely influenced by our experiences, environment, and personal dedication. With practice, perseverance, and passion, we can harness our innate abilities to achieve remarkable feats and make meaningful contributions to the world around us. Whether it's through honing our artistic skills, honing our leadership abilities, or honing our interpersonal talents, embracing and developing our natural gifts enriches not only our own lives but also the lives of those around us.

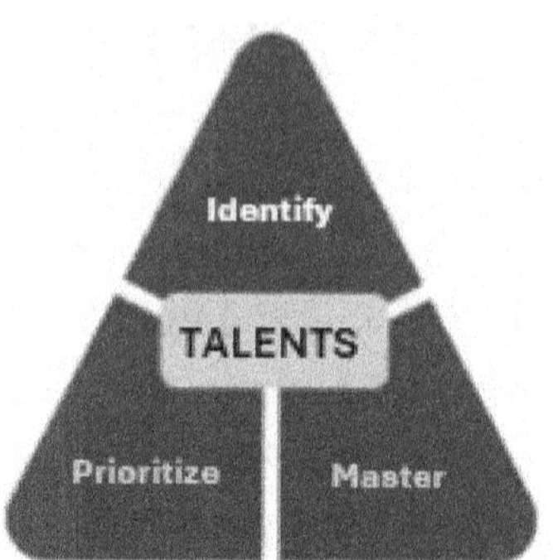

Identify
TALENTS
Prioritize
Master

Identify

Identifying our natural talents can be an exciting journey of self-discovery, akin to embarking on a treasure hunt where the prize is a deeper understanding of ourselves. One of the first steps in this process is **paying attention** to the activities that bring us joy and fulfillment. Whether it's effortlessly picking up a musical instrument and creating harmonious melodies or effortlessly solving complex puzzles, these moments of flow often point to areas where our natural talents lie. By observing our interests, passions, and inclinations, we can uncover clues about our inherent abilities and strengths.

Another valuable strategy for identifying our natural talents is **seeking feedback** from those around us. Friends, family members, teachers, and mentors can offer valuable insights into our unique gifts and aptitudes. They may notice patterns in our behavior, such as our knack for empathizing with others, our flair for storytelling, or our aptitude for problem-solving, that we might overlook ourselves. Their observations can provide valuable validation and encouragement as we navigate our journey of self-discovery, helping us recognize and embrace our innate talents with confidence and clarity.

Engaging in a variety of experiences and activities can also shed light on our natural talents. Trying out new hobbies, exploring different subjects, and challenging ourselves in unfamiliar domains can uncover hidden talents we never knew we had. Stepping outside our comfort zones allows us to stretch our abilities, uncover new passions, and unlock previously untapped potential. Through experimentation and exploration, we can cultivate a deeper awareness of our natural talents and harness them to lead more fulfilling and purposeful lives.

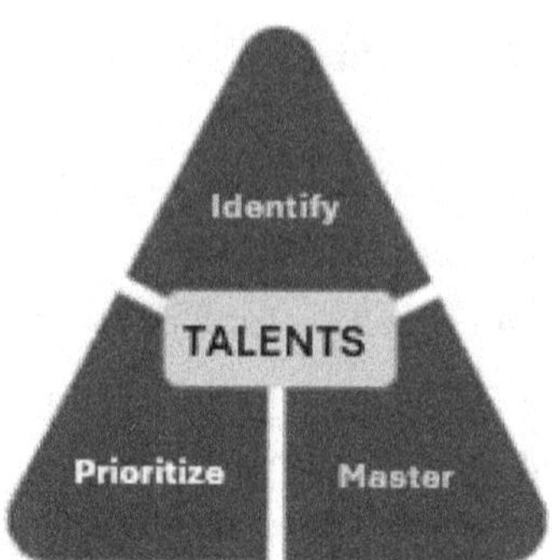
Identify
TALENTS
Prioritize
Master

Prioritize

Prioritizing where we spend our time and energy is like being the director of our own life movie, ensuring that each scene contributes meaningfully to the overarching storyline. Just as we carefully choose which activities to fill our days with, deciding **where to invest our precious time and energy** is crucial for cultivating a life that reflects our values, goals, and aspirations. By prioritizing wisely, we can create a sense of balance and fulfillment that enriches our lives and enhances our overall well-being.

One of the key benefits of prioritizing our time and energy is that it allows us to **focus on what truly matters most to us**. With so many demands competing for our attention in today's fast-paced world, it's easy to get caught up in a whirlwind of busyness, leaving us feeling drained and disconnected from our true passions and priorities. By consciously allocating our resources to the people, activities, and pursuits that align with our values and goals, we can cultivate a sense of purpose and direction that guides us toward greater fulfillment and satisfaction.

Finally, prioritizing where we spend our time and energy enables us to **achieve greater efficiency and effectiveness in pursuing our goals.** Just as a skilled chef carefully selects the finest ingredients to create a delicious meal, we can optimize our productivity by focusing on the tasks and projects that offer the greatest return on investment. By identifying our top priorities and devoting our energy to them wholeheartedly, we can maximize our impact and create meaningful outcomes that resonate with our values and aspirations. In doing so, we can experience a greater sense of accomplishment and fulfillment, knowing that we are channeling our resources toward what truly matters most in our lives.

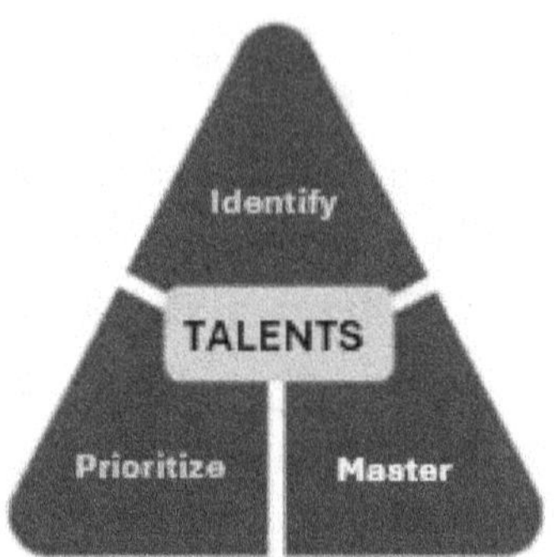

Identify
TALENTS
Prioritize
Master

Master

Mastering a natural talent is like unlocking a hidden superpower within ourselves, unleashing our full potential and opening doors to endless possibilities. Whether it's playing a musical instrument, excelling in a sport, or honing a creative skill, dedicating time and effort to mastering our innate abilities can have profound benefits for our personal growth and fulfillment. By **investing in the development of our natural talents**, we not only enhance our skills and expertise but also cultivate a deeper sense of self-confidence and satisfaction.

One of the greatest advantages of mastering a natural talent is the **sense of fulfillment and accomplishment** it brings. There's a special joy that comes from seeing our hard work and dedication pay off as we progress from novice to expert in our chosen pursuit. Whether it's mastering a difficult piece of music, perfecting a challenging yoga pose, or creating a masterpiece with our artistic talents, each milestone reached fills us with a sense of pride and satisfaction, fueling our passion and motivation to continue striving for excellence.

Moreover, mastering a natural talent **opens up new opportunities** for personal and professional growth. As we refine our skills and expertise, we become better equipped to tackle challenges, seize opportunities, and pursue our goals with confidence and determination. Whether it's advancing in our career, pursuing new hobbies and interests, or making meaningful contributions to our communities, the mastery of our natural talents empowers us to make a positive impact in the world around us. By embracing our innate abilities and committing ourselves to their development, we not only enrich our own lives but also inspire others to unleash their own potential and pursue their dreams with passion and purpose.

Having a natural talent is not enough. We have to turn a natural talent into a "skill that pays the bills!" I may have the natural talent of remembering numbers but it is necessary to develop that into an accounting job or any job related to numbers. Like balancing a spread sheet, analyzing a profit and loss statement, etc. So, get out there and turn your talents into skills that can support you through life.

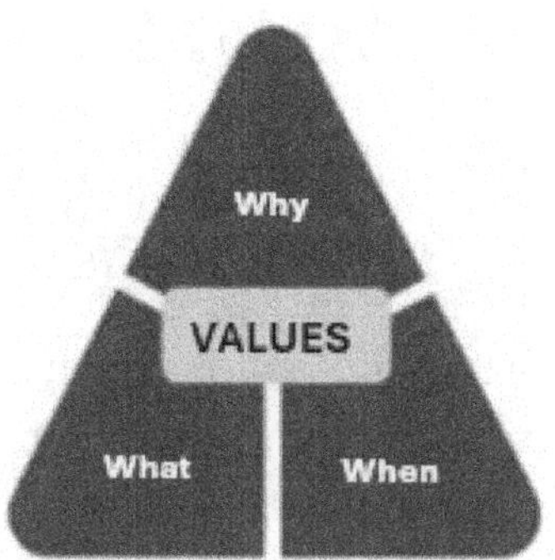

VALUES

Values are deeply personal and can vary greatly from person to person. Here's a list of common values that many people hold dear:

1. **Honesty**: Being truthful and sincere in all interactions.
2. **Integrity**: Acting in alignment with one's moral principles and ethical standards.
3. **Respect**: Treating oneself and others with dignity, courtesy, and consideration.
4. **Compassion**: Showing empathy, kindness, and understanding towards others.
5. **Gratitude**: Appreciating and acknowledging the blessings and positive aspects of life.
6. **Courage**: Facing challenges and adversity with bravery and determination.
7. **Authenticity**: Being genuine, sincere, and true to oneself.
8. **Resilience**: Bouncing back from setbacks and adversity with strength and perseverance.
9. **Empathy**: Understanding and sharing the feelings of others.
10. **Responsibility**: Taking ownership of one's actions, decisions, and obligations.
11. **Fairness**: Treating all individuals impartially and justly.
12. **Equality**: Believing in and advocating for equal rights and opportunities for all.
13. **Generosity**: Sharing one's time, resources, and talents with others.
14. **Open-mindedness**: Being receptive to new ideas, perspectives, and experiences.
15. **Tolerance**: Accepting and respecting differences in beliefs, opinions, and lifestyles.
16. **Peace**: Promoting harmony, cooperation, and non-violence.

17. **Freedom**: Valuing individual autonomy, liberty, and self-determination.
18. **Love**: Forming deep connections and caring relationships with others.
19. **Optimism**: Maintaining a positive outlook and believing in the possibility of a better future.
20. **Growth**: Pursuing personal development, learning, and self-improvement.

This is by no means an exhaustive list, as values are subjective and may vary depending on cultural, religious, and individual differences. Each person may prioritize these values differently based on their unique experiences, beliefs, and priorities.

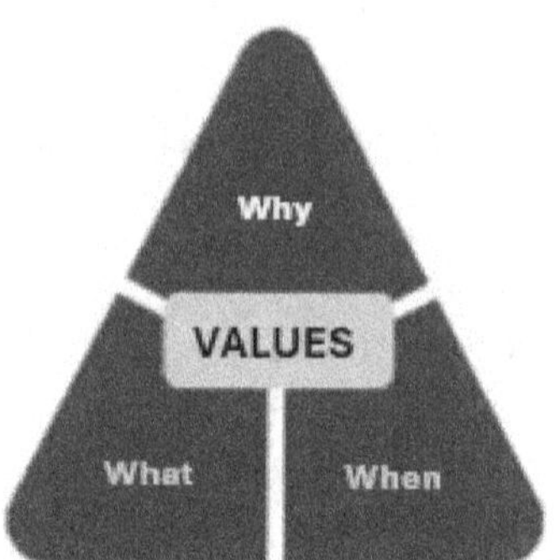
Why
VALUES
What
When

Why

The significance of why someone values something is deeply rooted in human psychology and personal experience. Value attribution is not merely about assigning worth to an object, idea, or person; it reflects an individual's beliefs, desires, and priorities. Understanding why someone values something offers profound insights into their identity, motivations, and aspirations.

Firstly, the things people value often **serve as anchors for their sense of self.** Whether it's a cherished possession, a principle they uphold, or a relationship they hold dear, these elements contribute to shaping one's identity. For instance, a person may value their family above all else because it represents their roots, their support system, and the source of their emotional fulfillment. By understanding why someone holds certain values dear, we gain a glimpse into the intricate layers of their personality and what matters most to them.

Secondly, values act as **guiding principles that influence decision-making and behavior.** When individuals align their actions with their deeply held values, they experience a sense of integrity and purpose. For instance, someone who values honesty will strive to be truthful in their interactions, even when faced with temptation or adversity. Recognizing the reasons behind someone's values provides valuable insights into their ethical framework and how they navigate the complexities of life.

Lastly, the importance of why someone values something lies in its role in **shaping relationships and fostering connections.** Shared values often form the foundation of meaningful bonds, whether it's friendship, romance, or collaboration. When individuals find common ground in their values, they establish a sense of rapport and mutual understanding that strengthens their connection. Moreover, respecting and acknowledging the values of others cultivates empathy and promotes harmonious interactions, fostering a sense of community and belonging.

Understanding why someone values something allows for deeper empathy and more meaningful relationships, ultimately enriching both personal and social dynamics. So, ask yourself, what is your "Why?"

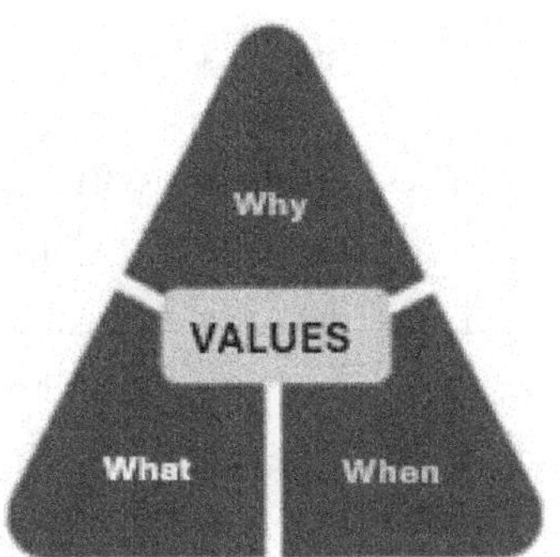
Why
VALUES
What
When

What

Focusing our energy and efforts on **what truly matters** is like shining a spotlight on the most meaningful aspects of our lives, illuminating the path to fulfillment and success. In a world filled with endless distractions and competing demands, it's easy to lose sight of our priorities and scatter our attention in a hundred different directions. However, by consciously directing our energy toward the people, activities, and pursuits that align with our values and goals, we can create a sense of purpose and clarity that guides us toward greater fulfillment and satisfaction.

One of the key benefits of focusing on where we spend our energy is the ability to **achieve greater effectiveness and efficiency in pursuing our goals.** Just as a laser beam concentrates light into a powerful, focused beam, focusing our energy allows us to channel our efforts toward the tasks and projects that offer the greatest return on investment. By identifying our top priorities and dedicating our time and attention to them wholeheartedly, we can make significant progress toward our objectives and create meaningful outcomes that resonate with our values and aspirations.

Moreover, focusing on what we should be spending our energy and efforts on enables us to **cultivate a deeper sense of fulfillment and well-being.** When we invest our energy in activities that bring us joy, fulfillment, and a sense of purpose, we experience a greater sense of satisfaction and contentment in our lives. Whether it's pursuing our passions, nurturing meaningful relationships, or making a positive impact in our communities, focusing on what truly matters allows us to lead more meaningful and fulfilling lives. By prioritizing our energy and efforts, we can create a life that is rich in purpose, joy, and fulfillment, where every moment is spent in pursuit of our highest aspirations and deepest values.

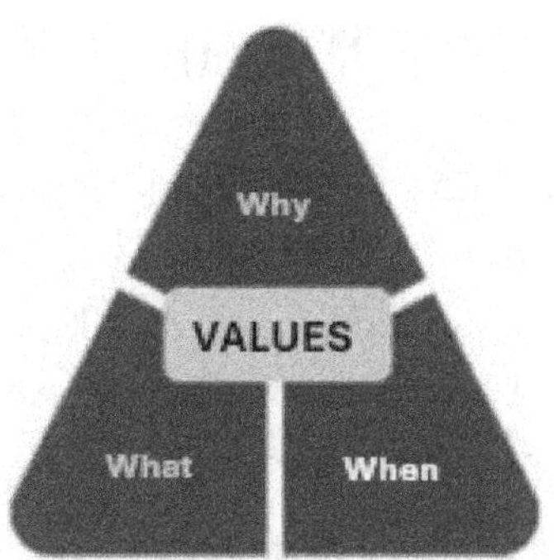
Why
VALUES
What
When

When

Overcoming procrastination is like unlocking a door to a world of limitless possibilities, where our dreams and aspirations await us on the other side. While procrastination may seem like a harmless habit at first, it can quickly snowball into a major obstacle standing between us and our goals. By tackling procrastination head-on, we reclaim control of our time and energy, paving the way for greater productivity, success, and fulfillment in all areas of our lives.

One of the most compelling reasons to overcome procrastination is the profound impact it can have on our personal and professional growth. When we procrastinate, we put off important tasks and responsibilities, delaying our progress and hindering our ability to reach our full potential. Whether it's starting a new project, pursuing a passion, or tackling a challenging goal, procrastination robs us of valuable time and opportunities for growth. By confronting procrastination and taking action in the present moment, we can break free from its grip and unlock our true potential to achieve remarkable feats and make meaningful contributions to the world around us.

Moreover, overcoming procrastination allows us to cultivate a greater sense of self-confidence and empowerment. When we consistently follow through on our commitments and take proactive steps toward our goals, we build trust in ourselves and our abilities. This newfound confidence fuels our motivation and drive, empowering us to overcome obstacles, persevere through setbacks, and achieve success in all areas of our lives. By conquering procrastination, we not only transform our habits but also strengthen our belief in our capacity to create the life we desire, one productive step at a time.

The best advice I ever got on this was to "run at your problem, not away from them" because what you resist...will persist!

Local
NEEDS
National
Global

NEEDS

The needs of the world are multifaceted and complex, spanning various domains including social, economic, environmental, and political spheres. Some of the most pressing needs that the world faces today include:

Basic Human Needs: Access to clean water, nutritious food, adequate shelter, and healthcare are fundamental requirements for human survival and well-being. Many communities around the world still lack these basic necessities, leading to widespread poverty, malnutrition, and preventable diseases.

Education: Quality education is essential for empowering individuals, reducing inequality, and fostering economic development. However, millions of children and adults worldwide still lack access to education due to factors such as poverty, conflict, and discrimination.

Healthcare: Ensuring access to affordable and quality healthcare services is crucial for promoting public health and reducing mortality rates. Addressing healthcare disparities, improving infrastructure, and expanding healthcare coverage are key priorities for global health initiatives.

Environmental Sustainability: Climate change, pollution, deforestation, and loss of biodiversity pose significant threats to the planet and future generations. Protecting natural resources, promoting renewable energy, and adopting sustainable practices are essential for mitigating environmental degradation and preserving ecosystems.

Peace and Security: Conflict, violence, and instability continue to plague many regions, causing immense human suffering and hindering development efforts. Promoting peacebuilding, conflict resolution, and respect for human rights are critical for achieving lasting peace and security.

Economic Development: Addressing poverty, unemployment, and economic inequality is essential for promoting inclusive growth and prosperity. Investing in infrastructure, job creation, and entrepreneurship can stimulate economic development and improve livelihoods for marginalized communities.

Social Justice and Equality: Combatting discrimination, inequality, and social injustices is vital for building inclusive and cohesive societies. Upholding human rights, promoting gender equality, and advocating for marginalized groups are central to achieving social justice and equality.

Technology and Innovation: Harnessing the power of technology and innovation can drive progress across various sectors, from healthcare and education to agriculture and energy. Closing the digital divide, fostering technological advancements, and promoting innovation are crucial for addressing global challenges and improving quality of life.

Addressing these needs requires collective action, collaboration, and sustained efforts from governments, civil society organizations, businesses, and individuals worldwide. By prioritizing these challenges and working together to find innovative solutions, we can create a more equitable, sustainable, and prosperous world for all.

The question to answer now is...what is your appetite in finding needs and filling them with your skills? Is it local? Or national? Or global?

Local
NEEDS
National
Global

Local

Fulfilling the needs of a local community is like stitching together a quilt of support and solidarity, weaving threads of compassion and care to create a tapestry of belonging and resilience. One of the most compelling reasons to address the needs of our local community is the opportunity to make a tangible, immediate impact on the lives of our neighbors and fellow citizens. Whether it's providing food assistance to families facing hunger, offering educational resources to students in underserved schools, or supporting local businesses and entrepreneurs, meeting the needs of our community fosters a sense of connection and solidarity that strengthens the social fabric and enriches the lives of everyone involved.

Addressing the needs of a local community promotes economic vitality and sustainability by fostering a thriving ecosystem of businesses, services, and resources. When we support local enterprises and initiatives, we create opportunities for economic growth, job creation, and entrepreneurship, driving prosperity and vitality throughout the community. By prioritizing local sourcing, sustainable practices, and equitable distribution of resources, we can build a resilient and inclusive economy that benefits everyone, from small business owners and workers to consumers and residents.

Meeting the needs of a local community builds trust, cohesion, and resilience among residents, creating a sense of belonging and shared responsibility that transcends individual differences and challenges. When we come together to address common needs and concerns, we forge bonds of solidarity and mutual support that empower us to weather adversity and thrive in the face of uncertainty. By nurturing a culture of collaboration, empathy, and reciprocity, we create a community where everyone feels valued, supported, and empowered to contribute their talents and resources toward the collective good, creating a brighter, more resilient future for all.

Local
NEEDS
National
Global

National

Addressing national issues is like working together to mend the fabric of society, stitching together solutions that benefit the entire nation and pave the way for a brighter future. One of the most compelling reasons to focus on national issues is the opportunity to create positive change that transcends individual communities and regions, impacting the lives of millions of people across the country. Whether it's tackling issues such as poverty, inequality, or environmental degradation, addressing national challenges requires collective action, collaboration, and commitment from all sectors of society to create lasting solutions that promote the well-being and prosperity of all citizens.

Also, addressing national issues fosters a sense of unity and solidarity among citizens, inspiring individuals to come together to work towards common goals and aspirations. When people from diverse backgrounds and perspectives join forces to address shared challenges, they build bridges of understanding and empathy that transcend differences and create a sense of belonging and cohesion. By fostering a culture of cooperation, mutual respect, and inclusivity, addressing national issues strengthens the social fabric of the nation, forging bonds of solidarity that empower citizens to work together to build a brighter, more equitable future for all.

Finally, addressing national issues promotes progress and innovation by harnessing the collective ingenuity, creativity, and expertise of individuals and organizations across the country. When stakeholders from government, academia, business, and civil society collaborate to address pressing national challenges, they bring together diverse perspectives, ideas, and resources to develop innovative solutions that drive meaningful change and impact. By fostering an environment of innovation, collaboration, and forward-thinking, addressing national issues stimulates economic growth, social development, and technological advancement, paving the way for a more prosperous and sustainable future for generations to come.

Local
NEEDS
National
Global

Global

Working on a global level presents a myriad of exciting opportunities for individuals to make a meaningful impact on a worldwide scale. One of the primary advantages of working at a global level is the ability to address pressing issues and challenges that transcend national borders. Whether it's combating climate change, promoting human rights, or advancing global health initiatives, working on a global stage allows individuals to contribute to solutions that affect the lives of people in every corner of the globe, fostering collaboration and solidarity among nations and cultures.

Additionally, working on a global level offers unparalleled opportunities for cultural exchange and learning. By engaging with individuals and organizations from diverse backgrounds and regions, individuals gain valuable insights into different perspectives, traditions, and ways of life. Whether it's through international collaborations, cross-cultural partnerships, or global conferences and events, working on a global level fosters a spirit of mutual understanding and cooperation that transcends cultural barriers, paving the way for greater empathy, tolerance, and interconnectedness among people around the world.

Working on a global level provides individuals with a platform to drive innovation and positive change on a grand scale. From pioneering scientific research and technological advancements to advocating for policy reforms and sustainable development initiatives, individuals working on a global stage have the opportunity to shape the future of humanity and leave a lasting legacy that extends far beyond their immediate surroundings. By harnessing the power of collaboration, creativity, and collective action, individuals can tackle some of the most pressing challenges facing humanity today, paving the way for a more equitable, sustainable, and prosperous world for future generations.

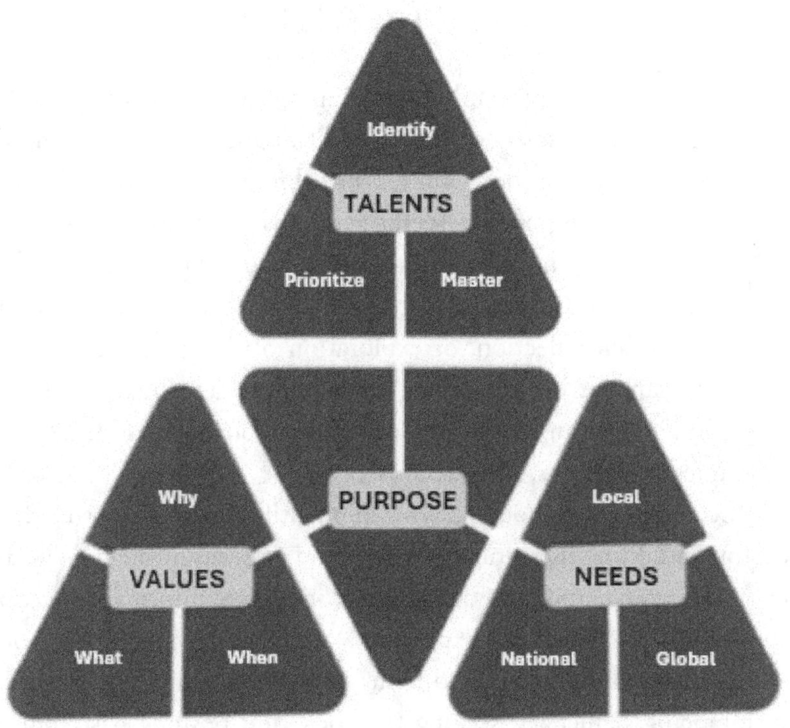
Identify
TALENTS
Prioritize
Master
Why
VALUES
What
When
PURPOSE
Local
NEEDS
National
Global

SUMMARY

Discovering, nurturing, and leveraging one's wheelhouse is like unlocking a treasure chest of innate abilities and passions, paving the way for a fulfilling and successful journey through life. The first step in this process is **finding one's wheelhouse** – that unique combination of strengths, interests, and talents that sets an individual apart and fuels their sense of purpose and fulfillment. Whether it's through introspection, self-reflection, or exploration of different activities and experiences, uncovering one's wheelhouse requires a willingness to listen to one's inner voice and follow the path that resonates most deeply with one's values, aspirations, and passions.

Once one's wheelhouse has been identified, the next step is to **develop and refine** these innate abilities and passions through dedicated practice, learning, and growth. Whether it's through formal education, mentorship, or hands-on experience, developing one's wheelhouse requires a commitment to continuous improvement and self-discovery. By embracing challenges, seeking feedback, and pushing past comfort zones, individuals can cultivate their talents and expertise, honing their skills and abilities to achieve mastery in their chosen pursuits.

Finally, applying one's wheelhouse involves putting one's talents, strengths, and passions **into action** to create meaningful impact and achieve personal and professional success. Whether it's pursuing a career that aligns with one's interests and abilities, contributing to causes that resonate with one's values, or leveraging one's skills and expertise to make a positive difference in the world, applying one's wheelhouse allows individuals to unleash their full potential and leave their mark on the world. By leveraging their unique strengths and passions, individuals can find fulfillment and success in their endeavors, while also making meaningful contributions to their communities and society as a whole.

Invitation

I heard a great analogy one time where the speaker compared an adult playing basketball against a five-year-old versus someone who had more experience and talent. The former doesn't do anything for you while the latter expands your boundaries to play faster and smarter. It helps you grow, in other words.

My invitation to you is to find opportunities to help you grow intellectually, emotionally, physically, spiritually and so on. By putting ourselves in challenging situations, we get to stretch our boundaries and see how far we can go with something. There is a "big hit" when we've accomplished something that we never thought possible before. And as the saying goes "Life is lived outside your comfort zone."

Another suggestion that I learned from experience is not to spend too much time going around looking for your purpose. The chance of you bumping into something that turns into a life project are slim to none. For instance, it is rare for someone to say, "When I was twelve years old, I saw a veterinarian save a dog's life and from then on, I knew I wanted to be a vet." Instead...create your purpose. Spend all the time you need studying, research and developing a blueprint of what you think would give you fulfillment. And as you go along, tweak your plan and develop your wheelhouse.

I didn't know till I was 50 years old what I wanted to do career-wise. I had spent the previous 25 years being the best husband and father I knew to be but my vocation was really secondary at that time. Now that I'm actively retired, my focus is on philanthropy. So, over time my purpose changed. I wanted good grades in school, then I wanted a healthy family life. My career became a focus after the kids left home and now I'm enjoying my golden years doing what I love to do...teaching the Tryune Concept.

Since you know that life works in threes, begin applying this concept and watch your life soar!

When you're with someone who is sharing their struggles with you...just smile at him/her and give them one of these. He/she will ask "What is that?" Then simply reply "Life Works in Threes."

Other titles coming out:

- Weight Struggles?
- Abundance Struggles?
- Parenting Struggles?
- Romance Struggles?
- Life Struggles?
- Happiness Struggles?
- Sales Struggles?
- Speaker Struggles?
- Time Struggles?
- Network Struggles?
- Marriage Struggles?
- Divorce Struggles?
- Money Struggles?
- Career Struggles?
- Dating Struggles?
- Caretaker Struggles?
- Forgiveness Struggles?
- Grieving Struggles?
- Success Struggles?
- Golf Struggles?
- Workplace Struggles?
- Stress Struggles?
- Shame/Guilt Struggles?
- Addiction Struggles?

Quotes about Purpose

"The two most important days in your life are the day you are born and the day you find out why." - Mark Twain

"The purpose of life is a life of purpose." - Robert Byrne

"The purpose of life...is to enjoy it." - Dalai Lama

"When you find your why, you find a way to make it happen." - Eric Thomas

"Life is never made unbearable by circumstances, but only by lack of meaning and purpose." - Viktor Frankl

Remember,

When you get right down to it,

Life is about making choices.

Every day, all day long, that's what we do.

- *We choose to get out of bed or not.*
- *We choose to clean up or not.*
- *We choose what to eat all day.*
- *We choose to exercise or not.*
- *We choose to go to work or not.*
- *We choose to do a good job or not.*
- *We choose to come home or not.*
- *We choose to watch TV or do something constructive.*
- *We choose to bed at a decent hour or not.*

And the next day...we start all over again.

What is the meaning of this? Get good at choosing.

Before you can get good at choosing though...you need to understand how life works in threes.

When someone is struggling with a particular area or two, chances are they are "out of

balance" with how life works. How does life work? Life works in threes.

If you're interested in personal topics like life, health, money or business topics like sales, time management and public speaking...TRYUNE WORKS! can shed some light on creating success in those areas.

The definition of TRIUNE is a group of three things; united. Being three in one, such as - humans are *mental, physical* and *spiritual beings.* The word TRYUNE is a play of the word TRIUNE, encouraging all to try this concept and help eliminate struggling unnecessarily.

LifeWorksInThrees.com